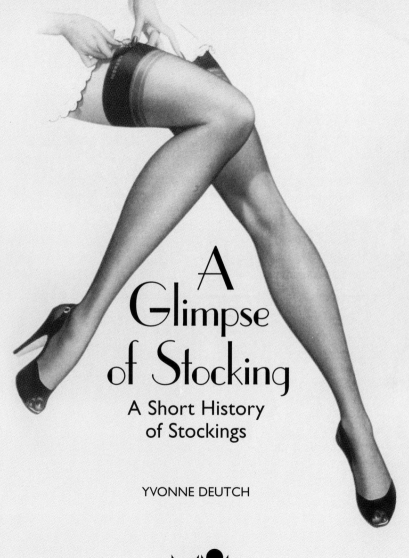

A
Glimpse
of Stocking

A Short History
of Stockings

YVONNE DEUTCH

First published in Great Britain in 2002 by
Michael O'Mara Books Limited
9 Lion Yard
Tremadoc Road
London SW4 7NQ

Copyright © Michael O'Mara Books Ltd, 2002

A CIP catalogue record for this book is available from the British Library

ISBN 1-85479-422-1

1 3 5 7 9 10 8 6 4 2

www.mombooks.com

Designed and typeset by Design 23

Printed and bound in Singapore by Tien Wah Press

Picture acknowledgements:
Getty Images: 8, 9, 21,31, 32, 33. 34, 35, 36,38, 44, 46, 47, 51, 55
The Advertising Archive: 1, 3, 15, 16,18, 22, 23, 24, 28, 41, 50
The Mary Evans Picture Library: 12, 20

Contents

In olden days...

As a woman quickly shimmies into her stretch tights or smooths a pair of filmy stockings over her legs, she's unlikely to be musing about how these essential items came into being. She'll know that the tights and stockings that she's wearing now have been mass produced by machine, of course. But she may not be aware that the basic skills that enabled her legwear to be manufactured on these hi-tech machines date back as far as the Stone Age.

Ancient hosiery

It took thousands of years for humans to learn how to spin yarn and then to weave and knit it into fabric. Weaving is a process of interlacing yarn to create a fabric, and was probably invented by the ancient Egyptians. Knitting – a more complicated skill that produces a fabric from interlocking loops of a continuous strand of yarn – came afterwards; this is the origin of the basic process by which modern-day tights and stockings are made.

Early samples of genuine hand knitting were excavated from the site of the ruins of the ancient Syrian city, Dura Europos. The city was originally founded in 280 BC, and eventually became an ethnic melting pot in which Greeks, Byzantines, Persians, Christians and Jews lived and worked side by side until the Persians attacked and destroyed the city around AD 256. In 1928 excavations uncovered three small fragments of knitted fabric.

In Egypt the archaeologist Sir W.M. Petrie discovered a knitted, brown wool sock (probably dating from the fourth century AD) and another hand knitted from wool yarn that had been dyed purple. A child's wool sock made with alternating stripes of red and yellow yarn was yet another miraculously preserved find. One of the socks that Petrie unearthed had even been darned – a hauntingly touching detail of domestic economy. No one knows precisely how long knitting had been established in Egypt, but by the time the country was conquered by the Arabs in AD 641, the craft was thriving. From this strong base it is very likely that knitting was introduced to Spain as part of the spread of Islamic culture and know-how. Arabic influence was at its peak in Spain during the eleventh and twelfth centuries, and there is plenty of evidence that hand knitting was widely established as a valuable domestic skill there and throughout the rest of Europe by the thirteenth and fourteenth centuries.

It was men's legwear that underwent the greatest transformation. The long, flowing gowns inherited from classical times had been common to both sexes, but during the Middle Ages, men established a long-term preference for shorter garments down to the waist and increasingly tight coverings for their legs. Early on, these were made from shaped and sewn fabric, and were held up at the knee by some form of tie or garter. Knitted stockings in silk or wool were first noted in England around 1553, and knitting was commonly done by both men and women.

Those daring dandies
By the sixteenth century, men's legs were a major focus of creative self-expression. They often wore layers of colourful knitted socks and tight-fitting breeches in contrasting checked and striped patterns. The extravagant new fashion gave rise to

a brand new industry. Groups of highly skilled hand-knitters became established in various parts of the country to satisfy the booming demands of the hosiery market. By the end of the century, large quantities of stockings knitted from English wool were being exported to Germany, France, Italy, Holland, and Spain.

Fit for a queen

While her male subjects flaunted their legs in their exotic hosiery, Queen Elizabeth I had her own, highly refined fashion preference, as the following account indicates:

> In the second year of Queen Elizabeth, 1560, her silk woman, Mistress Montague, presented Her Majesty with a pair of black knit silk stockings for a new year's gift; the which, after a few days of wearing, pleased Her Highness so well that she sent for Mistress Montague and asked her where she had them, and if she could help her to any more; who answered, saying:
>
> 'I made them very carefully of purpose only for Your Majesty; and seeing these please you so well, I will presently get more in hand.'
>
> 'Do so,' quoth the Queen, 'for indeed I like silk stockings so well, because they are pleasant, fine and delicate, that henceforth I will wear no more cloth stockings.'
>
> And from that time unto her death the Queen never wore any more cloth hose, only silk stockings.
>
> Edmund Howes, The Annals or General Chronicles of England 1615

Ordinary female citizens had to be content with more humble versions. By the time Elizabeth had ascended the throne in 1558, well-made knitted stockings were widely available to women. In particular, the island of Jersey was justly renowned for its finely knitted woollen hose, known as 'Jersey stocks'. Women's stockings were characteristically knitted with integral 'clock' motifs, often situated close to the ankle, and had decorative detail on the seams. A chilling record of this fashion was noted on 8 February, 1587. On that day Mary, Queen of Scots, went to her execution wearing plain white Jersey stockings. Over these she wore a pair of contrasting blue socks with silver clock motifs.

An amazing invention

Elizabeth was well aware of the value of the stocking manufacturing trade that had developed and flourished during her reign, and appreciated its contribution to her treasury in the form of taxes. She also took account of vested interests such as those of the organized knitting guilds when considering applications for licences and patents from individuals who wished to set up business in the same trade.

In 1589, an English clergyman called William Lee wished to secure a patent to establish his amazing invention – a machine that made stockings. The earliest recorded sources indicate that Lee's machine was intended to be used specifically to make silk stockings – the luxury end of the market.

Imported silk stockings were very expensive, and the available numbers of home knitters were fully occupied with producing woollen stockings. In response to news of the perceived threat to their livelihood, the vested interests of the knitting guilds made their protests felt. Despite her renowned fondness for silk stockings, Elizabeth may have feared stirring up unrest, and is reputed to have commented 'I have too much love of my poor people who obtain their bread by the employment of knitting to give my money to forward an invention that will lead to their ruin, by depriving them of employment and thus make them beggars.' Lee's application was refused.

Determined to succeed

Lee persisted in trying to obtain permission to use his machine in England for years afterwards. Finally, he left to set up in the city of Rouen in France. In 1612 he signed a contract with a French partner to establish a company that would manufacture both silk and woollen stockings.

A dramatic transformation

What is indisputable is that, by the end of the seventeenth century, machines that were based on Lee's original invention were in extensive use all over England and in several European countries. This was an extraordinary achievement of sixteenth century technology. The stocking industry was unique in its level of technical transformation. This allowed it to respond to subsequent changes in fashions. Women's stockings, for instance, now reached to above or below the knee, and were secured with small, sash-like garters, buckled or tied. During the reign of Charles II in the late 1600s, these were brightly coloured, and made of silk (or wool for poorer folk).

Bless your cotton socks!

In the early seventeeth century, the majority of the New England settlers were wearing hand-knitted woollen stockings, only the wealthiest could afford silk hosiery. They were also very fortunate in finding perfect conditions for growing cotton, originating in the Jamestown colony of the south. This valuable product was exported back to Britain and other European countries of course; but in time, as the colonies flourished and the population expanded, stocking knitting machines were successfully smuggled into New England. It was in this region that the hosiery-making industry was established, despite the attempts of the British to protect their interests in stocking manufacture. The thriving US market became amply supplied from domestic sources; American makers had plenty of cotton and wool available, and both these yarns knitted

up into warm, hard-wearing stockings. Silk had to be imported, however, and was still a luxury item.

War, war, war!

Cotton cultivation became the basis of the one-crop slave-labour economy of the American south; it was also the major economic cause of the Civil War during which the manufacturing areas of the north were cut off from their supplies in the south. When the war ended in 1865, the New England textile industry (including the stocking manufacturers) moved south to be closer to their precious home-grown raw material. A new era had begun.

A glimpse of stocking

From the early 1700s to the 1920s, the role of stockings in both male and female fashions remained relatively low key. For several generations, men continued to display their legs in knee breeches worn with silk stockings, often embroidered with the familiar clock motif. Eventually, however, by 1790, knee breeches, stockings and buckled shoes gave way to pantaloons tucked into high riding boots, which ultimately evolved into modern trousers. Meanwhile, men's silk stockings gradually became replaced by woollen socks.

Strides in technology

During this period, new hosiery machines arrived on the scene. Jebediah Strutt made the first knitting frame using a rib stitch in 1758, and in 1816, Marc Isambard Brunel built a circular knitting machine that produced tubular fabric – ideal for making stockings. The use of knitting frames had became fairly widespread in England by the middle of the eighteenth century. Home operators worked for wholesalers, from whom they rented their machines; and this home-based industry easily supplied the demands of the hosiery market.

Georgian splendour

Wealthy women wore heavy, richly decorated dresses during the reign of George II (1727-60); these opulent creations were supported by wide hoops made of cane or rattan. With their gorgeous dresses, fashionable women wore stockings made from rich silk fabrics decorated with woven patterns or embroidered motifs. Their stockings were held up with garters at the knee, and they wore high-heeled shoes covered with silk to match each gown. By 1740, although white silk stockings were *de rigueur* for full dress occasions, coloured stockings were fashionable for day-to-day wear.

Delicate plants

Women's fashions of the Regency era during the reign of George III (1760-1820) were notably lighter and simpler than those of past decades, with gauzy lightweight fabrics in delicate designs and colours. Muslin was a widespread favourite – either plain or spotted. Fashions were inspired by Grecian themes; dresses clung softly to the body, and waistlines were raised to just below the bosom. This period was Jane Austen's heyday, of course, and few of her devoted readers will forget the anxious, fussing voice of Emma Woodhouse's father as he urges his sturdy offspring to look after her delicate health.

> 'Young ladies should take care of themselves. Young ladies are delicate plants. They should take care of their health and their complexion. My dear, did you change your stockings?'
>
> Emma, Jane Austen (1775-1817)

Essentially, the style of women's hosiery in Jane Austen's time had remained unchanged from previous decades, and our young heroine's stockings would have been made of white silk, to complement the delicate fabrics of her frocks. Many Regency women would have knitted their own stockings for informal wear – the craft of 'netting' (knitting) was considered to be a suitably useful and creative pastime for gentlewomen – and they knitted pretty 'stocking purses' as fashionable accessories, as well as their home-made hosiery.

Snappy garters

Few things would have been more tiresome than wearing stockings that constantly slipped down to the ankle. Garters were the only way of keeping stockings partially supported until the advent of suspenders. Originally, they were made from a narrow strip of knitted wool, and tied above the knee. This took advantage of the natural elasticity of wool fibres; but woollen garters were by no means perfect, as they soon lost their stretch. Inventors finally addressed their skills to solving this problem, and, early in the 1830s, some beautifully made garters appeared, made of tiny, brass wire springs encased within silk coverings. Later, garters made of elastic woven from india rubber were produced, and these had become widespread by the 1850s.

Victorian mode

During the Victorian era (1837-1901) the prevailing fashion decreed that respectable women should be clad in layers of clothing from head to foot — legs (and stockings) were nowhere to be seen — at least in public. The following description of a day out at the beach for a young, upper-class, American society lady of the 1890s provides a piquant flavour of the time:

> 'When I was seventeen my skirts almost touched the ground; it was considered immodest to wear them shorter. My dresses had high, tight, whalebone collars. A corset laced my waist to the eighteen inches fashion decreed. An enormous hat adorned with flowers, feathers and ribbons was fastened to my hair with long, steel pins, and a veil covered my face. Tight gloves pinched my hands and I carried a parasol. Thus attired, I went to Bailey's Beach for a morning bathe. There, clad in a blue alpaca outfit consisting of a dress under which were drawers and black silk stockings, with a large hat to protect me from the sun, I bobbed up and down over the incoming waves. Needless to add that I was never taught to swim'.
>
> The Glitter and the Gold, Consuelo Vanderbilt (1877-1964)

Colour codes

As the young Miss Vanderbilt aptly demonstrated, black stockings were required when wearing a dark-coloured or black dress. In general, Victorian women wore silk or cotton stockings in black or white (the silk versions often had cotton tops). However, during the 1860s, coloured stockings became fashionable, and styles dyed in shades that matched the wearer's dress even became acceptable for evening wear. During the 1870s and 1880s, openwork and embroidered stockings became a popular choice. For full-dress formal occasions, however, white silk was still deemed to be the only appropriate choice.

The naughty nineties

For generations, women's legs had been kept strictly 'under wraps' in polite society. Their display had somehow acquired a kind of taboo. During the last decade of Queen Victoria's reign, however, a distinct social change was under way. In some part, this was due to the influence of Edward, Prince of Wales, the king-in-waiting. He was the leader of a 'fast' pleasure-loving social set, and was notorious for his affairs with fashionable women, often from the theatre. In another sector of the theatre, the female stars of the popular music-halls had became notably daring and sexually titillating. Meanwhile, well-off gentlemen of the time could slip over to Paris and feast their eyes on the glamorous legs of the cancan dancers at the notorious Moulin Rouge.

The Edwardians

A new era beckoned with the accession of Edward VII to the throne in 1901 and it subtly changed the prevailing mood. The aristocratic ladies in the king's social set defined the tone and 'look' of the period. They favoured long, elegant dresses that were outrageously frivolous and feminine, made from exquisite fabrics trimmed with lavish decorations.

The dominant silhouette of these stylish Edwardian woman deliberately emphasized the bosom, often with the aid of a heavily frilled and boned camisole or bodice. Beneath these they wore special 'S'-shaped corsets to achieve this eminently desirable effect. These were fitted with suspenders that had metal clasps. Stockings were now made longer and reached well over the knee to the thigh; they were usually available in black or white – though, in 1912, a neutral beige colour was introduced.

The Gibson Girl

The same trend influenced women in the USA; followers of this shapely, womanly look were called 'Gibson Girls' (the style was first introduced into popular magazines by the American illustrator Charles Gibson). He highlighted blouses that

were lavishly decorated with layers of frothy lace, designed to emphasize the way the corset thrust the top half of the body forward. Women were thrusting forward in other ways, too.

America pioneered the way, as these 'Gibson Girls' clad in their fashionable corsets, started to enter the workplace in increasing numbers. Mass circulation magazines, printed clothes patterns, and mail-order catalogues from companies such as Montgomery Ward and Sears, Roebuck and Co. made it possible for ordinary women all over America to become aware of the latest styles. Mail order made it possible for them to purchase an entire wardrobe of clothes – including a full range of silk, lisle and woollen stockings, of course.

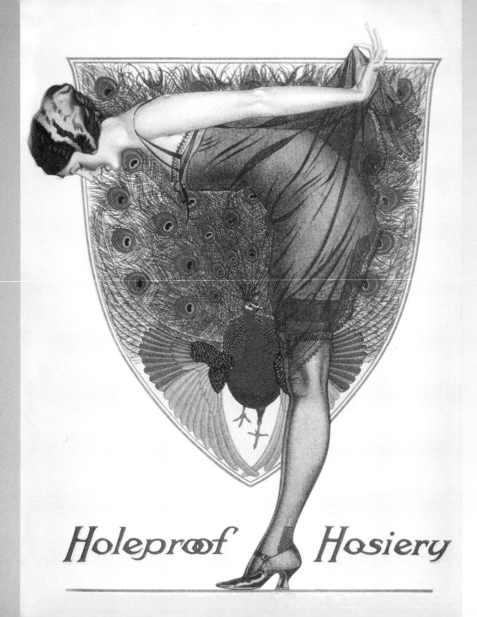

Holeproof Hosiery

Something shocking!

During the first half of the twentieth century, fashion design closely reflected trends in modern art. The evolving themes of the modern movement moved from the 'S' curved silhouette that reflected sinuous Art Nouveau styles to the first, radically simplified outline that arrived before the First World War. This trend continued throughout the 1920s, resulting in the silkily elegant, streamlined, body-hugging dresses of the 1930s.

The shock of the new

The Parisian designer Paul Poiret emerged as the leading influence on women's fashion after 1906 – his designs made that daring, crucial leap into modernism, and brought about a major revolution in women's clothing. He proclaimed that his styles expressed the independent spirit of contemporary women and reflected dramatic changes in attitudes. 'It was,' he declared, 'in the name of Liberty that I proclaimed the fall of the corset and the adoption of the brassiere which, since then, has won the day.' Out went exaggerated curves; they were now replaced by a longer, more fluid line. Poiret designed straight, almost tubular frocks that skimmed the body, featuring his trademark geometric patterned fabrics.

Prisoners of fashion

The new fashions did not really liberate women from wearing corsets; Poiret

simply devised one that flattened the hips to conform to his ideal, modernist tubular profile. These corsets reached almost to the knees, and made it rather difficult to sit down. Then, in 1910, Poiret sprang another surprise. He invented the hobble skirt – a style that harked back to the 'harem' skirts of the Middle East (he was entranced by Eastern patterns and colour schemes). His skirts became so narrow, women found it impossible to move freely. In fact, to avoid splitting the seams of their skirts, his dedicated fashion followers controlled the length of their stride by wearing a length of cord around their legs, confining themselves to a tiny shuffle. Poiret readily admitted, 'Yes, I freed the bust, but I shackled the leg.'

Best foot forward

One direct effect of the hobble look was that it focussed attention on women's feet in an unprecedented way – and the result of this was that shoes also became more exotic and colourful, teamed with pure silk stockings, to match the designs of the clothes.

The shock of war

The First World War had a rapidly sobering effect on the fashion industry, as severe restrictions were forced upon designers and wartime shortages made fabric scarce. A major consequence was that hemlines began to rise and women's legs were now definitely on view. However, these newly revealed legs were clad in eminently sensible shoes and stockings; silk had become a scarce commodity, so most women had to wear lisle or wool stockings. Lace-up boots came back into fashion, valued now for their sheer practicality. At the same time, clothes developed a tailored style, influenced by the military uniforms of the period.

The roaring twenties

After the war ended, an ecstatically bright, optimistic and frenetically energetic period followed. Youth was at a premium because so many young men had been killed during the war. As a result, the 'bright young things' literally hurled themselves into an endless round of pleasure, fuelled by the proliferation of jazz and wild dances such as the Charleston.

The beauty business

Meanwhile, the desire for glamour had become established as an important theme in the majority of women's lives – mainly due to the growing influence of the film industry and the exquisite clothes worn by universally adored female movie stars such as Clara Bow, Louise Brooks and Josephine Baker. Fashion magazines such as *Vogue, The Queen,* and *Harper's Bazaar* provided mass exposure for popular styles and fashions; and cosmetics became a major industry.

The fabulous flapper

The iconic 1920s style of the legendary Jazz age was the 'flapper' look – characterized by knee-length skirts, short hairstyles and low necklines. The effect of this was guaranteed to shock the establishment. But these styles were also deliberately targeted to attract the opposite sex: the shortage of young men created by the war resulted in women wearing blatantly enticing clothes. The impact of this on men was immense – the sight of beautiful young women confidently wearing fashions that showed their long, slender legs, knees and thighs as they got in and out of cars, or travelled around on trains and buses, was the epitome of glamour dressing in its most potent form. Women's legs had now become a gratifying new focus of sexual allure.

Leggy lovelies

With their new prosperity, a large section of the female population had access to pretty silk stockings and elegant shoes. Legs and feet had become important fashion items, and up-to-the minute short skirts enabled them to show these off to best advantage. Garters worn at the knee were introduced to add a touch of drama – and stocking shades were extended to new colours such as grey and flesh tones. Shoe styles were influenced by dance crazes like the Charleston; the classic dance shoe was a single-bar pump with a pointed toe, high-waisted heel, and a tiny covered button. But there were other, far more exotic designs available – after the discovery of King Tutankhamun's tomb in 1922, Egyptian themes appeared everywhere.

Grin and bare it

Sophisticated glamour is one thing; daring wildness another. Some women of the 1920s merrily used their new-found freedom to kick over the traces while kicking up their heels. They behaved more outrageously than ever before – they found it amusing to smoke, drink, use swear-words, put on outrageous make-up, and generally push against the limits of conventional behaviour. For the first time they bared their legs in public – and competed to show off their knees with calculated abandon.

Silk stockings disease

It would have been precisely these women who were vulnerable to the infamous 'silk stockings disease' first noted during the 1920s; the same symptoms re-emerged several generations later in the 1960s, with the advent of the mini-skirt. This condition – *erythrocyanosis frigida crurarum puellarum* – is caused by the chronic effects of exposure to the cold. Women who had poor circulation or were naturally sensitive to cold incurred damage to the skin surface of their legs. These became an unhealthy-looking blue colour in winter, and a florid red shade in summer under the glare of hot sun.

The big crash

Those high-spirited women of the late 1920s were thoroughly enjoying their flirtatious fling, and they were eagerly experimenting with all the latest fashions. As well as the characteristic 'flapper' look, the sporty but elegant chic of the French fashion designer 'Coco' Chanel exerted a huge influence on women's clothes. She

invented easy-to-wear cardigan-style suits, accessorized with bare, beautifully tanned legs and bobbed hair styles.

Women needed all the spirit they could muster to face the next great shock to their world: the New York stock market crash of 1929 precipitated the Depression – a period of economic downturn that haunted most of the 1930s. Unemployment soared to staggering levels – and men were generally given what jobs there were. In this grim climate, many women turned to the consolation of the movies, where they could experience all that lost glamour at one remove.

Rayon stockings

Luxuries such as silk stockings were now out of the question for all but the very rich; consequently, some women turned to rayon, the 'artificial silk' substitute that was made from cellulose fibre. This had originally been invented in France in 1884, but was first manufactured for commercial use in the United States in an effort to create a cheaper substitute for silk, which was both precious and expensive. While nothing could replace the luxury and delicacy of silk stockings, those knitted from rayon yarn gradually found their niche in the market.

The elegant thirties

Not everyone was poor in the 1930s. The period saw the most shocking extremes of affluence and poverty. And the fashion industry held its ground surprisingly well, mainly thanks to the creative genius of designers such as Madeleine Vionnet, who dominated the period. Vionnet's greatest contribution to fashion was her discovery of the bias cut. This made fabric cling to the body and move naturally with it, creating her trademark look of subtly draped, graceful clothing.

Madame Vionnet used barefoot models to present her first solo collection, which was a typical exercise in her brand of unparalleled elegance. Inspired by the dancer Isadora Duncan, she dispensed with all corsets and constricting undergarments – and her beautiful clothes looked their best with pure silk stockings and beautiful shoes of course – both tantalizingly out of reach for the ordinary woman. What these women could not know was that scientists had already made a discovery that was to transform the world – they had invented nylon.

Will-ó-the-Wisp

BY MUNSTER

Now, heaven knows!

In 1937 the Du Pont company of America filed a patent on an amazing new material called nylon. A team of company scientists headed by Wallace Carothers had discovered that a tough, hard-wearing, flexible fibre could be created from coal tar, air and water. They developed a molten polymer from these elements that could be drawn into filaments, then cooled and stretched to form an immensely strong but transparent yarn. At last, researchers had produced a material that had the desirable sheerness of silk combined with astonishing strength. In their press release, Du Pont announced that, among its many predicted uses, nylon would be of 'revolutionary importance in fine hosiery' and that it could be 'fashioned into filaments as strong as steel, as fine as the spider's web, yet more elastic than any of the common natural fibers and possessing a beautiful luster.' For American women, this sounded like a dream come true!

The rush to buy

When the first nylons went on sale at stores throughout the USA in May 1940, four million pairs sold out in four days. In New York City alone, over 72,000 pairs were bought on the first day. Women everywhere were wildly enthusiastic about the new miracle fibre, and their demands amounted to big business – stocking manufacturers catered to a huge sector of the market. Clearly, anything that could realistically compete with silk was bound to succeed.

Ein Wunder

die bedri - Nade

zum Maschenheben

War again

Meanwhile, other forces were at work in the wider world. On 3 September, 1939 England and France declared war on Germany, which would change the way women dressed yet again. In 1940 most commodities were scarce in Britain, and luxuries such as silk stockings became virtually unattainable. The government asked the nation to 'make do and

mend'. Women's magazines offered advice on how to transform old clothes into modern styles. Fabric shortages meant that hemlines were at the knee; the fashion was for short skirts, sensible shoes and square-shouldered jackets that echoed the tailoring of uniforms – these were the classic components of wartime 'utility' clothes. Underclothes were just as utilitarian; plain briefs and a bra, or a combination of both, were worn with a petticoat. Corsets and similar foundation garments were no longer manufactured, since the rubber needed to elasticate them was diverted to the war effort.

Painted legs

With their legs clearly on view but with no pretty silk stockings to show them off, women still wanted to emulate their enticing glamour. Consequently, they tried painting their legs with the various brands of leg make-up that appeared on the market. They even created 'faux' seams, by drawing them down the back of each leg with eyebrow pencil. Working-class women who couldn't afford leg make-up tried various ingenious substitutes from the kitchen cupboard such as coffee and gravy colouring.

A brave face

In 1941 British women were called out to work to help the war effort and they toiled heroically in the munitions, tank and aircraft factories. Even so, they took enormous pride in their appearance and became skilled at improvising with make-up and hairdos. They even made pretty handbags with a hidden compartment to hide their gas masks. It would have been considered unpatriotic not to try and look one's best, even though the bombs were falling all around and the cities were burning.

Some women found virtue in tough, rueful irony, as shown in this extract from a poem of Dorothy L. Sayers:

> If it were not for the war
> This war
> Would suit me down to the ground...
>
> I need not buy new clothes
> Or change for dinner
> Or bother to make up my face —
> It is virtuous to refrain from these things.
> I need not shiver in silk stockings;
> I had a hunch about wool before it was rationed;
> Now I have knitted myself woollen stockings that come a long way up...
> As it happens, I like knitting
> And nothing gratifies one more
> Than to be admired for doing what one likes.
>   From London calling: Lord, I thank Thee

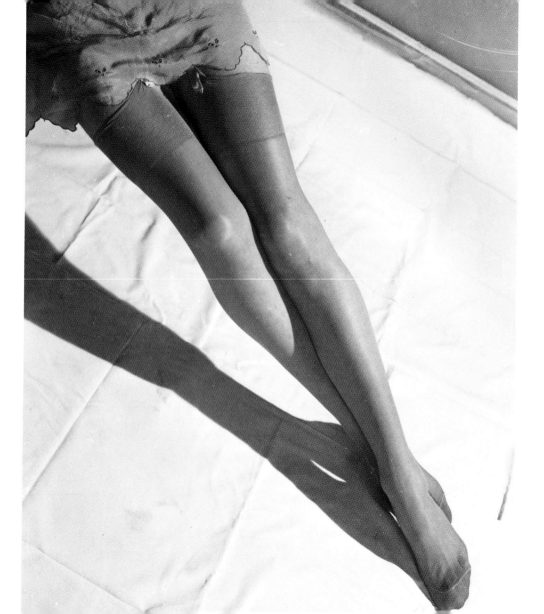

The rustling of silk

America didn't officially enter the war until 8 December, 1941. However, as early as July that year, it was already becoming clear that trouble was brewing – and this included conflict with Japan. The USA imported most of its supply of raw silk from Japan, and 90 per cent of that was used to make women's stockings. It was immediately clear that, if the supply of silk ceased, so would the manufacture of silk stockings. As soon as they became aware of this, American women panicked en masse. Thousands rushed straight out to the shops and headed for for the nearest stocking counter.

Avoid piggishness

The result was mayhem. Queues of determined women packed the aisles of the nation's department stores. Many demanded to buy two years supplies of silk stockings on the spot. It was reported

that, in Denver, one woman slapped three $100 bills on the counter and said. 'That many stockings, size nine, I don't care what color.' Stores roped off their stocking counters and employed muscular 'heavies' to head off the tide of women laying siege to their counters. Official pleas to 'avoid piggishness' fell on deaf ears. Then, in the first week of August, the US government announced that they would take over all existing stocks of raw silk for the production of parachutes and silk bags for explosives. By now, the rush to stock up had reached such panic stations that stores had to limit customers to two or three pairs each. But even this move failed to prevent a virtual sell-out throughout the USA by the end of that week.

Nylons to the rescue?

Silk stockings were certainly the item that women craved most but, once they were firmly cut off from supplies of these, most of them accepted the inevitable and allowed themselves to explore the appeal of nylons. These were still a comparatively new product, and had occupied a relatively small part of the market – as little as 20 per cent of total sales. But as they began to filter into the catastrophic gap left by the disappearance of silk, there was a period of temporary calm as women learned to enjoy the new substitute. This was to be short-lived, however. Within six months, the next blow came. In February 1942, the news was announced that the entire production of Du Pont's nylon supply was to be commandeered by the US War Production Board and used to make parachutes, powder containers, and other military products.

A bitter pill

The loss of nylon created an unsolvable dilemma for stocking manufacturers. They knew precisely what their typical woman customer wanted – filmy-sheer, delicate stockings that would make her legs look beautifully smooth and inviting to touch. Perhaps the unconscious message to men was that this was what the rest of her body was like; in any case, only silk and nylon stockings created the desired effect, made her feel wonderful, and at her most alluring. Nothing else could satisfy the powerful feminine craving for that particular kind of glamour.

Leg appeal

The symbolic status of sheer stockings was perfectly demonstrated by film star

Betty Grable, who was famous for her beautiful legs. She publicly peeled off her nylons at a war bond rally and they were auctioned off for $40,000. Betty Grable's name immediately comes to mind when the subject of beautiful legs arises. But she was part of a long tradition of leggy stars who appeared in popular musicals from the 1930s to the 1950s. With her sunny good looks and stunningly beautiful legs, she became the most popular pin-up among US servicemen during the war years. Her legs were insured for a quarter of a million dollars (although this figure was exaggerated to a full million by studio hype).

She, and other stars such as Ginger Rogers, Rita Hayworth and Marlene Dietrich, established women's legs as a new focus of alluring appeal – powered by sheer sexual drama and energy. Dancers in musicals wore long stockings that reached far above the tops of their legs; usually, these were specially made, long 'opera hose' that were either pinned or stitched onto their briefs, or secured high inside the briefs with extra suspenders.

An uphill task

Meanwhile, manufacturers struggled to satisfy the yearnings of their female customers. They had no silk or nylon at their disposal, so they simply tried their best to make do with the other yarn sources available to them – mainly rayon and cotton. But they knew they faced an uphill task. One discouraged producer commented, 'We could figure a way to knit them of grass one day, and the next day there would be a priority on grass.' Would rayon be the answer? Unfortunately not! The finest rayon that would have made the most acceptable stockings was quickly reserved for the war effort. The inferior quality rayon stockings that were put on the market were a bitter disappointment; they had no elasticity, they sagged and bagged in unattractive folds. What's more, they laddered easily, and certainly didn't have that elusive 'sheen' that made the skin beneath look so pretty and enticing.

Bobby socks

As for cotton, the best that even the finest 'natural shade' lisle yarns could do was to make a woman look like a blue-stocking as opposed to a belle. Realizing this, manufacturer's opted for the novelty approach; they produced cotton stockings in a range of colours, including green, pink, yellow, brown and black. Then they experimented with patterns – and women tried wearing stripes, checks, polka dots, appliquéd designs and motifs on their legs. Girls in the youngest age group began to opt out of grown-up fashion completely. They invented their very own, distinctively teenage American style, and wore casual, boyish clothes. They favoured short cotton socks worn with flat shoes, big sweaters and blue jeans.

Bootlegged!

Just like their European sisters, older, more sophisticated women in the US sighed for nylons, but because none were legally available, they tried all the usual strategies – they painted their legs, and pencilled in false seams with eyebrow pencil. As the war progressed, the more weak-willed were simply unable to resist the temptation to buy their stockings on the black market. These came from various sources; some were legally made for the US government, and strictly reserved for overseas. Others were manufactured from hijacked sources of raw nylon that was officially designated for the war effort.

Phony nylons

Some bootleggers preferred the more personal approach. Women would be furtively offered nylons that had appeared by mistake on a delivery van or, alternatively, that may have 'fallen off the back of a lorry'. Offices and waiting rooms of dentists and doctors were favourite choices for such secretive sales pitches. In addition to these illegally manufactured stockings, many racketeers made a huge profit from selling phony goods. They sold stockings that were not even made of nylon – marketed under names such as 'Mexican nylon', these usually turned out to be made of rayon.

Chocolates and nylons

A similar black market operated in Europe of course. No recollections of the war years are complete without stories of handsome GI's wooing luxury-starved women with gifts of nylons and candy; in fact, these two commodities became a substantial currency in themselves – the bargaining power of a chocolate bar and a pair of nylons was a considerable asset to the average GI. In fact, stockings were used in more serious areas of bargaining. It was discovered that US agents overseas could use a few dozen pairs of sheer nylons to obtain secret intelligence from cooperative women in Europe and North Africa. The women informers valued them more than money – since there was nothing to buy in the empty shops of war-stricken Europe.

Exquisite stockings in pure silk and nylon

KAYSER BONDOR

PRINCESS SLIPS IN 7 SIZES · LINGERIE · HOUSECOATS · BRASSIERES

Anything goes!

One of the most telling results of a post-war survey taken in the American city of Tulsa was that twice as many women reported that they had missed nylons than those who said they had missed men. So it is not surprising that, when the war ended in 1945, they were literally desperate to get their hands on those longed-for luxuries. The aftermath of war brought nylons back into US shops, but not fast enough. Now the streets of America witnessed the drama of domestic stockings wars; Macy's of New York City sold out its entire stock of 50,000 pairs of nylons in six hours. Meanwhile, in Pittsburgh, Pennsylvania, it was reported that 40,000 women waited all night in a downpour to buy nylons from a small hosiery store. Despite their hunger for smooth, nylon-clad legs, it was not until about 1948 that US production of nylon stockings to reached the promised post-war levels. Finally, those much-touted, brand new stocking-making machines had begun to purr into action.

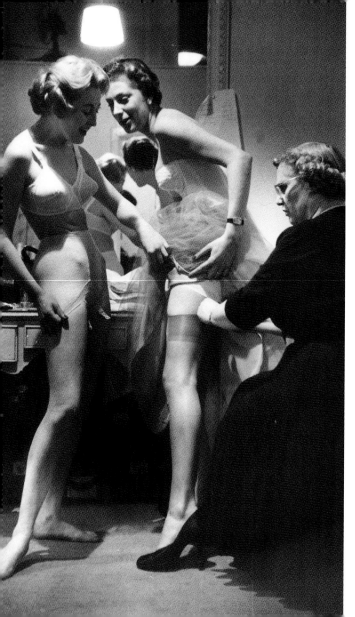

Rationing in Europe

Meanwhile, back in post-war Europe, there was hardly any let-up on the restrictions and hardships imposed throughout the years of conflict. Most consumer goods were severely rationed – and life was still very spartan. On the other hand, peacetime had arrived, soldiers had returned from the battlefield, and people could look forward to building a future once more. As for the availability of nylons, in the years immediately after the war, the only ones available were those that were handed out by an obliging GI, or from friends in the USA who sent them as gifts. Nylon had been manufactured in Britain during the war, but only to make parachutes and other military items. However, British producers knew that there would be a post-war demand for nylon stockings, and a team was sent to the USA in 1945 to conduct an intensive survey of the latest manufacturing techniques. They found that US suppliers had already made considerable advances, both in the creation of finer yarns that resulted in increasingly fine, gossamer-like stockings, and in the core machine technology.

Nylon spivs

Eventually, by 1946, nylons were manufactured in Britain for the first time, but for a long while they were in short supply on the domestic market. Most were exported, so that they could generate much needed money for the economy. Inevitably, this

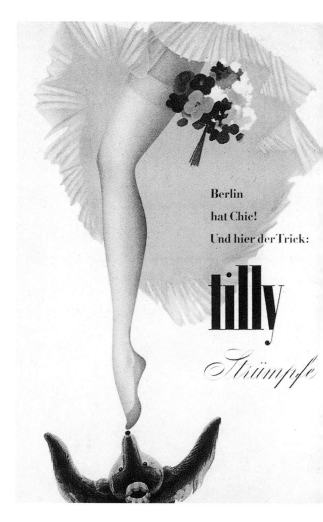

Berlin hat Chic! Und hier der Trick:

tilly Strümpfe

resulted in a thriving black market. During the early 1950s, newspapers frequently carried headlines such as £20,000 PROFIT IN NYLONS PLOT; or LINER LINK IN NYLONS RACKET. Racketeers were either 'diverting' supplies of nylons meant for overseas markets, or were smuggling them in from the United States. Shady characters from the back streets of London's Bayswater and Paddington were regularly gaoled for conspiracy to defraud the Customs and Excise department.

The New Look

Predictably, women's fashions changed dramatically after the war, reflecting their need to express the more overt levels of femininity that had been set aside while working in factories and munitions plants. In 1947, the French designer Christian Dior announced his 'New Look'; this featured longer lengths and fuller skirts, and heralded a return to womanly curves, emphasized by a narrow waist. The designer deliberately used generous quantities of fabric in these clothes to celebrate a new sense of lavishness and frivolity. The result was a soft, feminine and romantic look – often, starched cotton or nylon net half petticoats were worn under the full skirts. To achieve the shape required by these designs, special long-line bras were designed to shape the bosom and nip in the waistline. These were worn with light suspender belts, which eliminated the need for full-length elasticated corsets.

Fully fashioned

The pretty new styles were ideal for displaying beautiful legs; and once nylons became more widely available, women were at last able to relax and enjoy them. Most preferred the look of the classic 'fully fashioned' nylons that had an elegant seam at the back, defining the shape of the leg with the characteristic seam. These were the archetypal, iconic nylons that immediately conjure up visions of glamorous 1950s women constantly looking at their legs to check that their seams were straight. Many men felt that this concentrated attention on the legs, with the frequent adjustment of stocking seams, was profoundly sexy. Consequently, fully fashioned nylons gained a widespread reputation for generating a distinctly erotic 'charge'.

Knit to fit

Stockings were manufactured in plain, white nylon yarn, and were dyed to the required colour afterwards. There were many variants of light and dark beige and brown shades, but 'American Tan' was a universally favoured colour. It gave the illusion that the wearer had healthily tanned legs. Each nylon had to be meticulously knitted and sewn to a specific foot size. At that time, if you wanted to buy a pair of nylons, you had to ask for your particular size, just like shoes.

Fashionable circles

The 'flat knit' process of making stockings was not the most economical method, as it involved a considerable amount of time and effort in the detailed finishing. This introduced significant labour costs into the manufacturing process; it also meant that a lot of stock was lost because handling the stockings increased the chances of damage. The alternative method was to knit stockings on circular machines that were able to create a single, seamless tubular stocking. This was shaped to the leg by tightening the stitches, but the result was not always completely successful – many women found that these stockings 'bagged' at the ankle because they did not fit properly.

Seamless progress

The earliest versions of circular knitting machines had been in existence since the 1930s. With technical improvements, however, the new machines were able to produce stockings much faster than their fully fashioned counterparts – moreover, they were much smaller and cheaper than the huge flat knit machines. A decorative seam could be added to the stocking after it had been made, if required, though the fashion for wearing seamless nylons became increasingly popular. While the main appeal of these stockings was their lower cost, many women actively preferred the seamless look, and felt liberated from the need to constantly check whether their seams were straight. In any case, by the middle of the 1960s, the fully fashioned market was thoroughly eclipsed by seamless stockings. But even then, the problem of having to produce stockings in individual foot sizes had not been resolved.

The big stretch

The solution to this problem was already waiting in the wings. Early in the 1960s, stocking manufacturers had begun to introduce a newly improved technology that allowed them to add 'memory' to stocking yarn. They created an attractively sheer 'stretch fibre' that was able to expand and then snap back to its original shape without distortion. This was as revolutionary as the discovery of nylon; it meant that stockings could be made in one size, but would expand to fit the contours of any woman's leg. At last there was a perfect answer to the problem of catering for all those different foot sizes. This was a major milestone for the hosiery industry – manufacturers and retailers moved quickly to promote their wonderful new product, which made buying a pair of stockings as simple as purchasing a can of beans. They also displayed them in bright, tempting new packaging, which made them even more of a 'fun-to-buy' product.

Suspender belts

Stockings still had to be held up with suspenders, of course, though even these had been revolutionized by the new 'stretch fibre' technology. During the early years of the 1960s, many women had been converted to the advantages of wearing 'roll-ons' with built in suspenders; these were comfortable, easy-to-wear girdles made from stretch fabric with no nasty bones that stuck into tender flesh and left unsightly marks on the skin. Roll-ons created a soft, natural body shape without being uncomfortably constricting.

They were also comparatively inexpensive, and easy to launder, providing comfort, convenience and economy in one simple formula that was perfectly in tune with the mood of the times.

LINGERIE, BAS

Ciel de France

Put the blame on Mame!

So, what was the mood of the moment during the 1960s? Essentially, it was one of sheer optimism and the joy of youth. Young people completely dominated the fashions and culture of the time. The post-war Baby Boom had created millions of teenagers who now entered this decade with astounding energy. Their tastes were major influences on every aspect of life, they pursued fun, freedom, exploration and experimentation, in everything from clothes to music. With such exuberance, it is not surprising that they went to extremes – for instance, young girls zipped through a dizzying array of fashion styles, including psychedelia, pop art, hot-pants, culottes, baby-doll and, most famous of all, the mini-skirt.

Swinging London

In an intriguing echo of the 1920s, hemlines had gradually became noticeably shorter in the 1960s. But while they had reached just above the knee in the 20s, by 1966, with the arrival of the mini-skirt, they had soared to an unprecedented mid-thigh level. It was the young London designer, Mary Quant, who pioneered the archetypal 'dolly bird' look – and it was the waif-like, young London model Twiggy who became its living icon. During that year every major fashion

magazine showed stunning photographs of the bright young things of the 1960s clad in ever briefer mini-skirts. Whether or not they had the perfect body to wear the style, most young women found the mini-skirt irresistible; it expressed the very essence of what they felt – a sense of fun, energy, freedom, sexual self-confidence and a cheeky sense of humour. Moreover, jobs were plentiful, and these youngsters had plenty of money to spend in the plethora of new clothes boutiques that sprang up all over London – from King's Road to Carnaby Street. For a magic moment in time, London was the true capital of the world of the young. And, beneath every fashionable mini-skirt, young girls were stepping out in another revolutionary fashion item – tights.

Bear necessities

How did tights find their unique place on the fashion scene? As usual, the answer is based on a convergence of numerous background influences. One of earliest of these was certainly the demands of the theatre; all those showbiz lovelies in popular musicals needed to have stockings that reached all the way up their legs and beyond, and classical ballet dancers needed suitable leg coverings as well. One British hosiery expert recalled that Bear Brand, the fully fashioned nylons producer, supplied the Bolshoi Ballet company with specially made tights during the 1950s. These were made on the company's fully fashioned machines, in thick, sixty-denier nylon.

Auntie Mame

The same company also received a special request for the star of the famous 1950s play *Auntie Mame*. The star of the show (Beatrice Lillie) spent most of the play in bed, and the request was for a leg covering that would look completely 'natural' when she got out of bed, but still protected her modesty. After some

experimentation with different thicknesses of yarn, Bear Brand managed to come up with a solution – flesh-coloured thirty denier tights – made from the finest nylon yarn they could use to make the tights on their fully fashioned machines. As *Auntie Mame* was due to have a long run, Bear Brand made quite a lot of these prototype tights; they then found that other people in the theatre were clamouring to have some for themselves. Inspired by this enthusiasm, the company decided to try and market their new product to the general public in 1957. The tights met with little response, however, and Bear Brand returned to their core market of selling fully fashioned nylons.

Tight technology

Back in the USA, during the late 1950s, stocking manufacturers were increasingly using circular knitting machines and were also experimenting with making early versions of tights. This process was far easier to accomplish with circular knitting machines. At first, the US hosiery manufacturers simply made each seamless stocking a little longer at the top; then, two stockings were paired up, and a slit was cut in the top inside leg of each to make the 'pantie' section. Finally, the two halves were simply sewn together. Gradually, the technique was refined, and tights eventually began filtering into the shops during the early 1960s. Clearly, every product has to respond to a widespread need if it is going to succeed – the fact that it was technologically easier to produce tights was not an answer in itself. The key to the creation of the demand for tights was the pace at which hemlines rose during the early 1960s; and this trend was derived from the wild energy of British street fashion.

The big freeze

Mary Quant may have put her official design hallmark on the mini-skirt in 1966; but the trend was there as early as the summer of 1963. And tights were already on hand at exactly the right time. Next came the freezing winter of 1963, and British girls resolutely refused to give up wearing their short skirts even though

Be as free as a bird. Leggy girl

Just slip into Berkshire pantie stockings and show the world a lovely leggy suspender-free leg . . . then walk free. Prices from 12/11 - 18/11.

in pantie stockings

BERKSHIRE B

temperatures plummeted. A few determined mini-skirted girls went about bare-legged in the freezing cold – and afterwards, some showed symptoms of the infamous 'silk stockings disease', *erythrocyanosis frigida crurarum puellarum*, first identified in the 1920s. Most girls gratefully clad their legs in the newly available tights, and found that these allowed them to wear their mini-skirts even shorter. There was no awkward gap of flesh to conceal at the top of stockings, and no suspenders to hide. As far as they were concerned, tights were utterly wonderful, and the sky was the limit.

Critical reviews

While young women breathed a sigh of relief at being freed from the bother of suspenders and stockings, thousands of men expressed their dismay at the abrupt disappearance of one of their favourite erotic zones – that enticing area of bare flesh just above the stocking top. In this case, however, the female passion for fashion ignored male desires, and young girls embraced tights with delight. Liberated in her mini-skirt, the British 'dolly bird' was the epitome of self-confidence. By 1970, the practical benefits of tights were being noted in newspaper headlines. One newspaper declared TIGHTS MAKE WOMEN BETTER DRIVERS. The reasoning behind the story was that, now they were freed from the constraints of girdles and suspenders, women were much more comfortable in tights, and could move their legs more easily. This made it possible for them to concentrate completely on driving, and therefore resulted in an overall improvement in their driving performance.

A tight fit

Even though women were generally enthralled with their wonderful new tights, there is no doubt that the early versions had real teething problems. Mostly, these were to do with achieving the right fit. The classic scenario, revisited many times in future hilarious sketches by women satirists, was of donning a pair of tights that either stretched up to the bosom, or pinioned the hapless wearer at the knees. However, as the makers realized the potential of their market, they made huge investments in improving their machinery and manufacturing processes; new technology was quickly developed to automatically cut, seam, stitch and sew perfectly made, properly sized tights. Meanwhile, those companies that had not recognized this seismic fashion change stayed with their fully fashioned machines, and continued making stockings. Inevitably, they found themselves at the wrong end of the market; although some older women continued to wear stockings, the young had voted overwhelmingly for tights.

Here to stay

Fashion is never static, and even the mini-skirt faded away in favour of maxi-skirts by the early 1970s. These longer skirt lengths did not persuade women to return to wearing stockings and suspenders, however. By this time, stockings claimed a mere 5 per cent of the market – a staggering slump from dominating 100 per cent of the market in the mid 1960s. But changing styles did create a new challenge for tights manufacturers. Once the technology of making tights was firmly established, companies all over the world had invested in the latest machinery. The key task from now on was that of creating a host of different textures, colours and weaves that reflected the shifting moods of fashion. For instance, the 'look' connected with the maxi skirt was that of an earthy 'back to nature' theme, and the fashion was for heavy, textured tights in a folk weave pattern. Then, throughout the

1970s, an array of patterned tights were produced. The most popular patterns were spots – either self coloured or in contrasting colours. The flood gates of experimentation with styles of tights had opened wide. Next came 'flock' tights, which had patterns embossed on the surface, and caused a great sensation. And they were to be followed by intricate lace patterns.

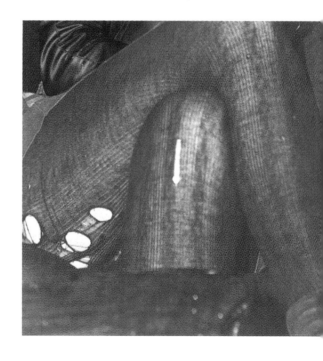

Punk

The definitive street style of the late 1970s was punk. The look was one of violent and extreme contrasts. Boys and girls wore their hair 'mohican' style – often dyed in vivid day-glo colours. The clothes they wore were just as shocking – ripped and torn, painted, safety-pinned, and accessorized with heavy metal chains. Many punk girls did something completely unexpected with tights – they favoured heavy black fishnets and often wore them as outer garments over their panties. The fishnets were strategically ripped to create gaping holes through which bare flesh could be viewed – almost as a mocking riposte to the archetypal image of female glamour.

Power and glory

Punk was not part of the mainstream however, and the major themes of fashions continued to evolve and change. The 1980s was an era of great prosperity – and women were gradually taking a greater part in corporate business at important management levels. In Britain, Margaret Thatcher, the first woman prime minister, was elected. It is no coincidence that this was the decade of power dressing, and during this period, many women wore quite formal outfits accessorized with smooth, increasingly sheer tights. These new tights had been made possible by the advent of the new stretch yarn, lycra, and this supplied both strength and amazing sheerness.

Sex appeal!

These tights were also sheer enough to be considered sexy, and this theme was taken up by the British company Pretty Polly. The company made a deliberate decision to transform the erotic 'image' of tights; for instance, in the early 1980s, the company's ads featured a wildly glamorous, long-legged model riding pillion on the back of a gleaming Harley Davidson. She was wearing sheer tights in a way that openly flaunted her sexual allure. In another interesting development, some women of the 1980s started taking an interest in wearing stockings again; this was an expression of deliberate sexual self-confidence and 'savvy' – these women knew exactly what they were doing. The market for stockings quietly crept up to around 16 per cent by the end of the decade, and settled there. In 1988, Pretty Polly put out a clever 'milestone' campaign on the fiftieth anniversary of Wallace Carother's historic discovery of nylon, featuring a new range of deliciously filmy stockings and tights that recalled the earlier luxury and glamour of nylons. The keynote of the moody, stylish, period-lit ad was 'NYLON BY WALLACE CAROTHERS; NYLONS BY PRETTY POLLY.' The message was that the new generation of tights and stockings not only had the classic sex appeal of the 1940s; they were also unprecedentedly soft and sensuous, and felt incredibly good on a woman's skin.

Colour me beautiful

The 1980s also saw the advent of a dazzling range of colourful tights, which emerged through the influence of French designers such as Chanel. Every outfit was subtly accessorised with a pair of toning tights – and these became available in myriads of colours. The famous Couture range featured 101 different colours – the company's advertising campaign used 101 girls to model each shade. They even lined up as living displays in the windows of major department stores – one such event at London's Debenham store literally stopped the traffic in Oxford Street.

By royal command

The same company had an unexpected coup in 1984. In common with every other tights manufacturer, they had been experimenting with every conceivable variety of decorative designs. These included embroidered motifs such as bows and butterflies. By fortunate coincidence, one of these designs was chosen by a beautiful young woman who was to exert the most astounding influence on fashion. Diana, Princess of Wales, was photographed wearing a pair of Couture's 'bow' tights – featuring a delicately embroidered bow at the ankle. The response was immediate and overwhelming – the company could not manufacture these tights quickly enough to meet the demand.

Back to black

At the end of the 1980s, the mini-skirt made a strong comeback – but this time it featured the magic fabric of the moment – lycra. These mini-skirts were truly body-hugging, showing every bump and bulge, and they were predominantly black. As for their matching tights, these were also black. The aim was to create a smooth, unified profile – tights were usually worn in an opaque black lycra to create this chic, unbroken line. This style exerted its influence right through to the 1990s – who will ever forget the desperate struggles of the decade's fictional heroine Bridget Jones, as she fought to stay slim enough to fit into her favourite short, black, lycra skirt and black tights? Her famous 'diary' struck a chord with millions of young women all over the world; they laughed (and cried) in sympathy.

Butterflies, bumblebees and crystals

Throughout the 1990s and into the new millennium, tights manufacturers have continued to develop endless ideas in their designs. For instance, in the late 1990s, Chanel showed models wearing fine fishnet tights with the designer's signature suits. These were immediately introduced into the market, and were very popular for about two years. The advent of technology that enables manufacturers to print images onto tights fabric has resulted in legs becoming moving picture galleries. The innovative company Sock Shop produced a dazzling range, including tartans, pony prints, leopard and tiger prints, Versace-style prints, and florals. The company has also put out 'paintings on legs' – tights that echoed the theme of major art exhibitions – including a Van Gogh tight, and a Marilyn Monroe image for a major pop-art show. Some tights are made to appeal to the luxury end of the market; new brides can purchase exquisite, hand-embroidered versions with appliquéd butterflies, bumblebees and flowers. And there are tights with thousands of crystal beads stitched on a side panel. As for the future, new innovations bring ever more new possibilities such as 'scratch and sniff' tights that release the customer's choice of perfume when the fabric is scratched. Whatever the mood of the moment, tights will be made available to match it.